Shhh!

By Jan Burchett and Sara Vogler
Illustrations by Jon Stuart

OXFORD
UNIVERSITY PRESS

In this story ...

💬 **TALK**

- Introduce children to the characters in this story: Max, Cat, Ant and Tiger.
- Point to the words that represent the characters' names and say each of the names together. Children will meet these words in the story.

Max

Cat

Ant

Tiger

Cat checks on the deck of the ship.

📖 READ

Then Cat heard a noise below. She looked down and saw Ant's toy ship.

She slid down some string and on to the deck with a thud.

"Found you!" she shouted excitedly to Max and Tiger.

👥 ACTIVITY

- Read out the following sentence: *Cat is on the deck*.
- Then ask children to write the sentence. Children could use magnetic letters, a whiteboard or a pencil and paper to write.
- Ask children to tell you which letter they would need to change in the word *deck* to make the word *duck*.
- **Have some fun!** If there is a group of children, play The Captain's Game. Ask children to pretend they are on a pirate ship. The captain gives commands (e.g. Scrub the decks!) and the rest of the children mime the actions. You could make the game more difficult by asking the captain to write the instructions!

READ

Cat climbed up on to Ant's desk. She found some fish, some shells and some pens.

She *still* could not find her friends.

ACTIVITY

- Point to the word *thick* on the page and ask children to count how many letters there are in the word.
- Then ask children to sound-talk the word *thick* (i.e. thick becomes th-i-ck).

shell

fish

thick pens

Cat checks on the desk.

READ

"Coming!" shouted Cat.

She looked around. "I wonder where the boys could be hiding," she said. She checked under Ant's bed. She found some trainers and a chess set.

But she could not find her friends.

I can not spot them.

chess set

READ

The four friends have special watches. When they push the buttons on their watches they can shrink to micro-size, like this …

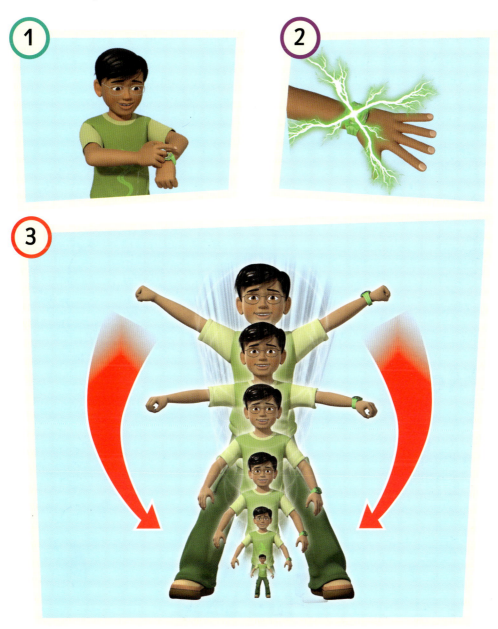

They become tiny and can have amazing adventures!

📖 READ

Max, Cat, Ant and Tiger were at Ant's house.

"Let's shrink and play hide and seek," said Max.

"That will be fun!" cried Cat. "You hide and I'll seek."

The friends pushed the buttons on their watches to shrink to micro-size.

Cat began to count: "One, two …"

👥 ACTIVITY

- Point to the word *ship* on the page and ask children to count how many letters there are in the word.
- Then ask children to sound-talk the word *ship* (i.e. ship becomes sh-i-p).
- Repeat the activity with the words *box* and *ball*.
- Max and Tiger are in the ship. Ask children to spot another object in the picture that contains the /sh/ sound. (fish)

⭐ Tip

See the inside back cover for more guidance on sounds.

READ

"Where is Ant hiding?" said Cat. "Where can he be?"

Max and Tiger would not tell.

Then, they all heard a noise. It was coming from the treasure box.

"Help! Help!"

It was Ant. He was stuck!

💬 TALK

- Talk about how children would feel if they were stuck somewhere and had to ask for help. Use this as an opportunity to extend children's vocabulary (e.g. scared, frightened).

👥 ACTIVITY

- Point to the word *check* on the page and ask children to sound-talk it (i.e. check becomes ch-e-ck).
- Then ask children to blend the sounds together and say the word (i.e. ch-e-ck becomes check).

READ

Max, Cat and Tiger pushed hard.

Finally – *POP* – the lid shot open and Cat helped Ant to climb out of the box. She had found all her friends at last!

 TALK

- Ask children to read the text on the page. Can they find two words that rhyme? (not, shot)
- Ask children to think of other words that rhyme with *not*.